# What Was a Cliché Before It Became One?

by Emma Carlson Berne

Consultant: Robert L. McConnell, PhD

CAPSTONE PRESS
a capstone imprint

Fact Finders Books are published by Capstone Press,
1710 Roe Crest Drive, North Mankato, Minnesota 56003
www.mycapstone.com

**Library of Congress Cataloging-in-Publication Data is available on the Library of
Congress website**
ISBN: 978-1-5157-6390-1 (library hardcover); 978-1-5157-6395-6 (paperback); 978-1-
5157-6407-6 (ebook)

**Editorial Credits:**
Michelle Bisson, editor; Bobbie Nuytten, designer; Tracy Cummins, media researcher;
Laura Manthe, production specialist

**Photo Credits:**
Alamy Stock Photo: CBW, 10 (top); iStockphoto: dovate, 14, JakeOlimb, 13,
pringletta, 16, RichVintage, 21; Shutterstock: A. and I. Kruk, 23, Amir Ridhwan, 24,
Andrey_Popov, 20, CHAjAMP, 9, Chettner Alexandru, 12, chrisdorney, 26 (top), Cory
Thoman, 7, Daxiao Productions, 28 (left), Dora Zett, 17, Hintau Aliaksei, 18 (left), Iurii
Kachkovskyi, cover (left), Julia Tim, 27, kstudija, cover and interior design element,
Lenushka2012, 10 (bottom), Malyugin, 5, MatiasDelCarmine, 15, nikolpetr, 18 (right),
Potapov Alexander, cover (right), spr, 11, Srijaroen, 22, VectorPot, 8, VikaSuh, 29,
Yayayoyo, 26 (bottom), Zastolskiy Victor, 4, Zerlina, 6

Printed in China.
010343F17

# Table of Contents

# CHAPTER ONE

# Clichés:
## Let's Call a Spade a Spade

**Clichés** are the elephant in the room. When your back is against the wall, it's hard to avoid clichés in your writing. They tend to turn up like a bad penny. You might find yourself using clichés willy-nilly. After all, they are alive and well in all of our writing. But with practice, you can learn to weed clichés out of your work—and you'll be a stronger writer as a result.

## Figurative Writing: Clichés

The paragraph above is riddled with clichés—familiar phrases that are comforting to use. Everyone knows what a cliché means. And clichés *can* explain a big idea in a just a few quick words—quick as a rabbit, in fact. (Sorry. Writers should try to avoid clichés like the plague, but sometimes they end up between a rock and a hard place. Yes, these are clichés too.)

**cliché**—phrase or expression that has been used many times and is familiar and stale

# What's in a Name?

## A Partial List of Clichés Involving Parts of the Body

- Nose to the grindstone

- Head in the clouds

- Nose in the air

- Apple of his eye

- Green thumb

- All thumbs

- Feet of clay

- Little pitchers have big ears

- Under my skin

- Costs an arm and a leg

- Break a leg

- Hairy eyeball

## Try It Out!

Can you figure out what these clichés mean? Get a piece of paper or grab your laptop. Then write down what you think these clichés mean. Then think of any other clichés involving body parts and write them down. See page 31 for the answer key.

Clichés are an example of figurative writing—most of the time, they don't mean exactly what they say. For instance, "She had my back against the wall" doesn't literally mean that a person had backed another person up against a wall. The phrase means that the person writing feels trapped. Figurative writing can make language fun. It can make a reader laugh or it can draw a strong image in a reader's mind.

Clichés can be idioms. An idiom is wording or phrasing that is specific to a particular language. "Getting in someone's hair" is an idiom. You *could* say "annoying someone" but that's a lot less descriptive. "Raining cats and dogs" is an example of an idiomatic phrase that is also a cliché. It's tired language and its phrasing is specific to English. If someone were to say "raining dogs and cats," you might know that the person is not a native speaker of English.

But clichés—like "he's a rotten egg"—can distract from good writing. They're tired-out phrases that don't spark the reader's imagination. When a reader sees a phrase they've heard so many times, it doesn't bring up a lively picture in his or her mind. Rotten eggs are very smelly and unpleasant, so calling someone a rotten egg would be a pretty bad insult. But because the phrase has been used too many times, the reader doesn't take note of the image you're trying to get across.

## Clichés from Various Parts of Life

Clichés *can* be pretty interesting, though. For one thing, there are so many. And they cover so many areas of life. Did you know, for example, that there are a whole slew of sea-faring-related clichés? "Anchors aweigh" means "let's go!" "Chock-a-block" is "stuffed full with no room." "Give a wide berth" means "give that person or object plenty of room." "High and dry" means "safe and sound" or "out of danger." There are clichés about sewing, clichés about food, clichés about the sun—in fact, clichés about everything under the sun, which is itself a cliché.

## Did You Know?

Phrasal clichés are sometimes called bromides. A bromide was an old-fashioned medicine that made the user sleepy. So using a tired-out, clichéd phrase—a bromide—might make your listener dull and sleepy.

Even the very best authors among us (or, one might say, *the best and the brightest*—sorry!), might use a cliché now and then on purpose, to make a point. "There's no great loss without some small gain," Ma Ingalls is always saying in *Little House on the Prairie*. Fern loved Wilbur "more than anything," the great master of prose, E.B. White, writes in *Charlotte's Web*. "Is this all *really* true?" Charlie Bucket asks his grandfather in Roald Dahl's *Charlie and the Chocolate Factory*. "Or are you pulling my leg?"

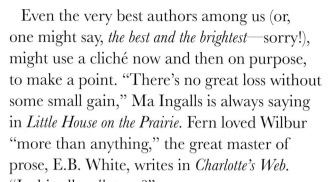

So don't feel bad if a cliché pops up every now and then (rats!) in your work. It's normal. It happens to all of us. And as you saw above, *sometimes* a cliché can help your writing. Use them sparingly though. The trick to getting rid of too many clichés is to be aware of them and root them out early, before they take hold and spread like nettles. After all, one bad apple can spoil a whole bin.

# When a Cliché Wasn't a Cliché

What's the origin of the French word, *cliché*? And why did we adopt it? Early in the 19th century, printers in France would use molten lead to make printing plates. They used the verb *clichér*, or "to click," to describe the sound created when a mold was dropped into molten lead. The printing plates themselves, which were also called *clichés*, were used over and over again in the same way. Gradually, the word *cliché* evolved to describe something used repetitively and without variation. That made it the perfect word to use, even in English, to describe tired language.

# CHAPTER TWO

# Clichés Over Time: History Repeats Itself

We're not used to thinking of proper word use as *fun*—more like an important skill to master in writing. But here is the fun thing about clichés.

*They weren't always.*

Some clichés used to be cool! For instance, going back to the nautical clichés, think of the phrase "all at sea." Someone might say, "I'm all at sea" when confronting a difficult math problem. The phrase means confused. Back in the olden days, a ship was referred to as "all at sea" when it was out of sight of land. And in the days before modern navigational tools, being out of sight of land was dangerous—and confusing. Nowadays, ships travel out of sight of land all the time, and use everything from radar to GPS to navigate. Being "all at sea" is no longer a confusing state to be in. But the phrase has stuck.

## Did You Know?

Eating "humble pie" may have come from eating "umbel pie." The umbels were the organs of an animal that had been butchered. The servants in colonial America had to eat this dish, while the master of the house ate the good pieces of meat.

Or how about the massive group of clichés related to agriculture and farming? You know, like "an apple never falls far from the tree"? Or having "an axe to grind"? Not too long ago, many people in this country would have understood the way in which ripe apples drop from apple trees in the fall. What about "beating a dead horse"? Your mom might tell you to stop "beating a dead horse" when you ask for a raise in your allowance again—after she has already told you no a hundred times before.

## Did You Know?

Just because a phrase is commonly used doesn't mean it's a cliché. "The day after tomorrow" is a good example. The phrase is used over and over, but there really isn't a better, more efficient way to identify the day that follows tomorrow!

# Bet You Didn't Know It's From Shakespeare

The poet and playwright William Shakespeare lived and wrote in 16th and 17th century England. He wrote 37 plays and 159 poems. Most of his plays are still well known, such as *Romeo and Juliet*, *Macbeth*, and *Hamlet*. Shakespeare's words were vivid, powerful, and colorful. In fact, it was he who first used many figurative phrases still in use today.

*For goodness' sake*

*Milk of human kindness*

*Jealousy is the green-eyed monster*

*In my mind's eye*

*Dead as a doornail*

*Brevity is the soul of wit*

*Forever and a day*

*One fell swoop*

*Bated breath*

*Good riddance*

## Reinvented Clichés

Some of the most fun clichés are **reinvented**. These clichés first were phrased one way, then gradually misspelled over time until they took on a nonsense meaning. It's like a centuries-long game of telephone. One interesting cliché in this group is the classic "melting pot" of U.S. citizenship. Most people know that this means that people of many different ethnicities and origins are swirled together in this country into a glorious stew of culture. But what fewer people know is that the phrase is based on a mistake. There's no such thing as a melting pot! In fact, the phrase was originally "*smelting pot*." A smelting pot is a pot in which various metals are melted together. Usually, the result is a metal that is stronger than its individual ingredients.

Which is an even better way to characterize America, when you think about it.

**reinvent**—to change something so that it appears to be entirely new

# Try It Out!

Using a separate sheet of paper, replace these clichés with fresh phrases of your own.

Black as night . . .

Red as blood . . .

White as snow . . .

Yellow as the sun . . .

Tired as a dog . . .

Mad as a hornet . . .

Happy as a clam . . .

# CHAPTER THREE

# Avoiding Clichés in Your Writing

No one is immune. All of us **succumb** to clichés sometimes, and all of us have to work hard to avoid them. Luckily, help is within reach.

The first thing to remember is that clichés tend to pop up when a writer is struggling. You know the feeling: you just *cannot* think of the right words. The next thing you know, your fingers are typing, "And in conclusion, it's worth mentioning that a bird in the hand is worth two in the bush." So be on the lookout. When you find clichés popping up like mushrooms after a rainstorm (ding! that's a cliché), stop. Look at your writing. Something isn't going well and you need to take a minute to figure out what it is.

**succumb**—to fail to resist pressure of some sort

# Try It Out!

The writer Karen Young wrote a paragraph full of clichés. Count how many you can find:

*"It was a dark and stormy night when suddenly a shot in the dark rang out. But like a tree that falls in the forest if no one hears, does the shot still count? The ricochet was obscured by the sudden downpour, as it began to rain cats and dogs. The parched earth was as dry as dust, absorbing the rain faster than the greased lightning that never strikes twice. Like a fool that rushes in where angels fear to tread, chanting, "I have nothing to fear but fear itself," I decided to go out in a blaze of glory. It was time to get the lead out and fight like a man."*

## Editing Your Writing for Clichés

Let's say you've sweated it out and you've finished your story or poem or history paper on colonial America. You might think you've avoided clichéd, boring writing. But you're wrong. Those little gnats are sneaky and they're in there, hiding. So the next task on your list should be to read your writing aloud to someone. Your mom or dad would be a good choice, as would an older brother or sister or friend. Have your reader raise his or her hand whenever he or she hears the cliché. Or, for more fun, get a little bell, like the kind in a shop, and have the reader ring it every time he or she hears a cliché. If that gets annoying, put away the bell. Instead, you can underline the cliché every time your reader hears one.

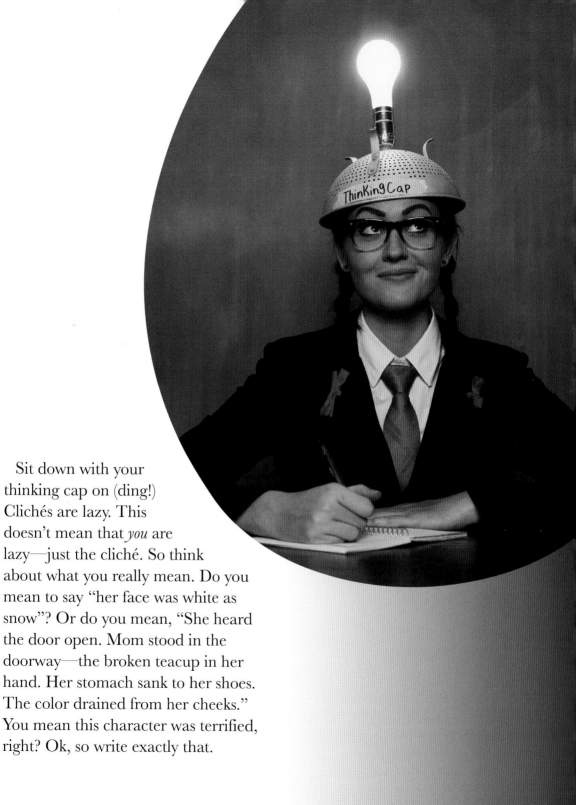

Sit down with your thinking cap on (ding!) Clichés are lazy. This doesn't mean that *you* are lazy—just the cliché. So think about what you really mean. Do you mean to say "her face was white as snow"? Or do you mean, "She heard the door open. Mom stood in the doorway—the broken teacup in her hand. Her stomach sank to her shoes. The color drained from her cheeks." You mean this character was terrified, right? Ok, so write exactly that.

## Preparation Is Key

Still struggling with clichés? Another possibility is that you haven't prepared enough before starting to write. Some fiction writers turn to clichés when they haven't thought enough about the character they're writing about: what he or she wants, why he or she wants something, how he or she would speak to another specific character. If you notice this happening in your writing, stop a moment. Take a breath. And then do a little extra thinking about the characters who are giving you trouble. Try one more time—without the clichés. The same is true when you're thinking about a nonfiction topic. Think about what you want to say, what your point is, and how best to say it.

Becoming a strong writer is hard. And it's not all magic notes and fairy dust. There are real, practical things you can do to improve your work. And it's not only students who need to work on improving their writing. It's everyone. Never let anyone tell you otherwise.

# CHAPTER FOUR

# Clichés in the Future:
## Time Waits for No Man

It can be exciting to think that the clever idiom of today is going to become the cliché of 2035. That's one of the most marvelous things about language—it's never **static**. It's always changing. Do you speak in Old English? Of course not—because our language has changed. Do you ever say to your friend, "Just between you, me, and the gatepost, Elizabeth gave Agnes the answers to that pop quiz"? That means the information should be kept secret. But you probably wouldn't use that particular cliché. It's pretty outdated.

## Try It Out!

Write a sentence with a cliché. Then write the same sentence expressing the idea contained in the cliché without using the cliché.

**static**—lacking in movement or change

# A Timeline of Clichés

**5th century–15th century (Middle Ages)** ) ... ( Rake over the coals—recalled the practice of dragging accused people over a bed of actual coals

**13th century** ) ... ( Get your just desserts—borrowed from the French verb for "deserve"

**17th century** ) ... ( Rule of thumb—refers to the many ways that thumbs can be used to measure things. Brewers might measure the temperature of their product by dipping in a thumb, for instance. Or you might measure the distance of something far away by holding up your thumb as a marker.

**19th century** ) ... ( black ball—used by men's social clubs. A white ball meant you were accepted, a black ball meant you were not.

**19th century** ) ... ( heard it through the grapevine—wires for the brand-new telegraph system reminded people of the wires used for grapes and their vines

## Modern Clichés

Those phrases that are quite hip now? Use them again and again and watch them **morph** into clichés before your very eyes. Social media is a particularly ripe picking ground for soon-to-be-clichés. Have you ever said "spoiler alert"? That used to be a cute way of saying, "We're going to give away the ending of that Netflix show!" Now, though . . . it just sounds tired. How about putting a **hashtag** on a cute phrase? #DontTellMeYouveNeverDoneIt. . . . It was linked to hashtags on Twitter, but then people were spinning them out and using them to say something else in their post. Now though, #ItsAsOldAstheHills.

#JUSTSAYING

**morph**—to change from one form to another

**hashtag**—word or phrase with the hash or pound (#) sign in front of it, used on social media

### Did You Know?

The French version of LOL (laughing out loud) is a little more extreme. They write MDR—*mort de rire,* which translates as "dying of laughter."

Texting has given us a whole new world (ding!) of clichés—some of them aren't even words. You text your friend, "Hey, I'm having the whole class over for a pool party!" And after that, you put a smiley emoji face. Cute, yes, but not particularly original. Or, the laughing-so-hard-I'm-crying face with the tears squeezing out of the eyes? Have you sent that, perhaps along with the text, "My mom is wearing her bellbottoms from the '70s right now!" OMG, people. I. Just. Cannot. No you didn't. THIS. All of those words are examples of new phrasing now that could become tomorrow's clichés.

## Evolving Language

There's usually a lot of hue and cry (ding!) about how some kind of modern invention is ruining our language. And don't be fooled, people, for "modern invention," read: youth. Not so long ago, people said that taking notes on a computer would cause all the youth of America to forget how to form proper thoughts. And yet, here you are, thinking! And there's been the usual **caterwauling** about texting, phones, and social media's effect on the language of our young people.

But, in fact, our beautiful language is in the same shape it's always been—alive, bright-eyed, and wriggling. Yes, sometimes we communicate in pictures of smiling emojis. But we're still writing. We're still *playing* with language. We're still having fun. Through the ups and downs, we're still standing. (Ding! Ding!)

**caterwaul**—make a shrill, wailing noise

# Try It Out!

Imagine three "clichés of the future."
Use these three scenarios:

**One** People have had iPhones implanted into their forearms.

**Two** People are primarily using self-driving cars.

**Three** Virtual-reality headsets are now the norm. Sometimes people wear them out onto the street.

# Glossary

**caterwaul** (CA-ter-wol)—make a shrill, wailing noise

**cliché** (kli-SHAY)—phrase or expression that has been used many times and is familiar and stale

**hashtag** (HASH-tag)—word or phrase with the hash or pound (#) sign in front of it, used on social media

**morph** (MORF)—to change from one form to another

**reinvent** (re-in-VENT)—to change something so that it appears to be entirely new

**static** (STAH-tik)—lacking in movement or change

**succumb** (seh-COME)—to fail to resist pressure of some sort

# Read More

Elliott, Rebecca. *Painless Grammar.* Hauppage, New York: Barron's Educational Series, 2016.

Fielder, Heidi. *The Know Nonsense Guide to Grammar: An Awesomely Fun Guide to the Way We Use Words!.* Lake Forest, Calif.: Walter Foster Jr, 2017.

*Grammar Rules.* Editors of Time for Kids! magazine. New York: Time for Kids, 2013.

## What's In a Name?

### A Partial List of Clichés Involving Parts of the Body from questions on page 5

- Nose to the grindstone—working persistently and hard without a break or without giving up
- Head in the clouds—dreamy and disconnected from reality
- Nose in the air—snooty or snobbish
- Apple of his eye—someone's special darling
- Green thumb—good at growing plants
- All thumbs—clumsy
- Feet of clay—making the same mistakes that all humans make sometimes
- Little pitchers have big ears—be careful, little children are listening and might hear something inappropriate in the adult conversation
- Under my skin—annoying
- Costs an arm and a leg—expensive
- Break a leg—good luck!
- Hairy eyeball—staring in a disapproving or pointed way

# Critical Thinking Questions

1. What is a cliché? Give two examples of a cliché from the text.

2. Why do you think the author placed the chapter discussing the future at the end of the book? How would the discussion be different if the chapter on the future was at the beginning of the book?

3. Find one example of a humorous cliché in the text and one example of a serious cliché. Study these, then write one humorous cliché and one serious cliché of your own.

# Internet Sites

Use FactHound to find Internet sites related to this book.

Visit *www.facthound.com*

Just type in 9781515763901 and go.

 Check out projects, games and lots more at **www.capstonekids.com**

# Index

2